Embellish Your Home

Embellish Your Home

by Dena

STERLING PUBLISHING CO., INC. NEW YORK
A STERLING/CHAPELLE BOOK

Chapelle, Ltd., Inc., P.O. Box 9252, Ogden, UT 84409
(801) 621-2777 • (801) 621-2788 Fax
e-mail: chapelle@chapelleltd.com
Web site: www.chapelleltd.com

Editor: Lisa Anderson
Book Design: Rose Sheifer
Photography: Ryne Hazen
Copy Editors: Jenn Gibbs, Marilyn Goff, and Michele Hollow
Production Assistant: Heidi Van Winkle

Library of Congress Cataloging-in-Publication Data

Fishbein, Dena.
  Embellish your home / Dena Fishbein.
      p. cm.
  " A Sterling/Chapelle Book."
  Includes index.
  ISBN 1-4027-2145-5
1. Handicraft. 2. Interior decoration--Amateurs' manuals. I. Title.

TT157.F54 2005
745.5--dc22

2005013853

10 9 8 7 6 5 4 3 2 1
Published by Sterling Publishing Co., Inc.
387 Park Avenue South, New York, NY 10016
©2005 by Dena Fishbein
Distributed in Canada by Sterling Publishing
c/o Canadian Manda Group, 165 Dufferin Street
Toronto, Ontario, Canada M6K 3H6
Distributed in Great Britain by Chrysalis Books Group PLC, The Chrysalis Building, Bramley Road, London W10 6SP, England
Distributed in Australia by Capricorn Link (Australia) Pty. Ltd.
P. O. Box 704, Windsor, NSW 2756, Australia
Printed and Bound in China
All Rights Reserved

Sterling ISBN 1-4027-2145-5

For information about custom editions, special sales, premium and corporate purchases, please contact Sterling Special Sales Department at 800-805-5489 or specialsales@sterlingpub.com.

Table of Contents

Introduction

I have a confession to make. When it comes to decorating my house, finding a gift, or buying clothes for my family, it's just not satisfying enough to pick an item off the shelf to use as-is. When I do, I feel there's something missing, something I don't want to live without. You could call it the personal touch or a bit of personal style.

In a world of convenience and speed, it can be too easy to lose our personal style. One way to get it back is by learning to embellish. Embellishing — turning the ordinary into the extraordinary — is a whole new way of shopping, looking at objects, and putting your stamp on them. It can be very quick and very easy; yet with the art of embellishing, you can transform everyday objects into one-of-a-kind treasures.

I was sixteen when I had one of my first turnaround projects. I'd found a cream-colored dress for 90% off its original price. It was gorgeous, it fit me perfectly, and it had a big stain down the front. I took it home, dyed it, changed out the buttons, and had a fantastic new dress for not much money and little imagination. There was no turning back after that: I was hooked on finding the potential in overlooked things.

Now, quite a few years later, I continue to transform anything from furniture to table settings, to light fixtures, to journals, to frames — The list goes on. My family even gets in on the act, and our home is filled with things that reflect the individuality of each of us.

With this book, I share with you some of the projects that we have enjoyed doing. All of them are simple enough to do with your kids, and I've given specific instructions to help you achieve satisfying results, whether you're a novice or a pro. As you begin, keep in mind that the best things to embellish might not seem like anything special at first. Remember to look past the surface of that ugly chair or outdated pillow and see if it has "good bones" — a solid foundation you can build on.

I hope this book inspires you to open your eyes to the endless possibilities for adding your personal touch to the world around you. Soon, you'll be finding your own ways to turn hand-me-downs and store purchases into personal expressions that fill your home with warmth and a style all your own.

Happy Embellishing!

Dena

Furniture

You might not know it yet, but your home is filled with hidden treasures. Go hunting and see what you can find! Old dressers, worn out chairs, tables with scuffmarks, and anything you may be holding onto just for sentimental reasons can be given new life through embellishing. The start of a project and each step of the way should be exciting and fun; and after it's done you will have an amazing piece of furniture and a wonderful sense of accomplishment.

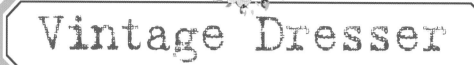

Vintage Dresser

There's nothing like the charm of an old wooden dresser—unless it's the charm of an old wooden dresser, embellished. This project started when my daughter Lisa, who loves vintage, wanted a dresser to suit her taste. By using vintage fabric along with paint, we added a new dimension of texture that enhances the nostalgic beauty of the original piece.

If you are intimidated at the thought of painting, don't worry. Remember, if you don't like what you've painted, you can always repaint or cover the area with fabric. The point is to enjoy the process, so relax and have fun!

Materials

- Old sturdy dresser
- Acrylic paints in a variety of colors
- Damp kitchen sponge
- Fabric adhesive
- Fabric scissors
- Foam brushes
- Gold fine-point marker
- Old toothbrush
- Palette
- Pencil
- Ruler
- Spray adhesive
- Sturdy vintage fabric to cover dresser panels
- Water
- White gesso

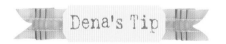
Dena's Tip

A gold marker is great for a project like this. You can get neat, straight lines with a ruler. If you have a steady hand, go for some nice curvy borders.

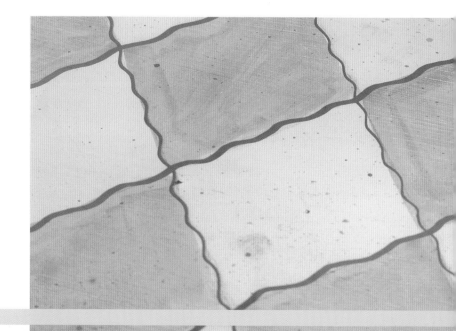

Directions

1. Cut vintage fabric to the size of panels plus ½" extra on all sides.

2. Paint the dresser with a base coat of gesso. Let it dry completely. Paint the background shades, using a damp sponge. (I used cream and forest green.)

3. If you feel inspired, paint a pretty landscape, a still-life scene, or other work of art on the front of the dresser. Let this dry.

4. Working with the vintage fabric, turn the extra ½" under and glue down with fabric adhesive to avoid frayed edges.

5. Spray the back of the fabric with the spray adhesive and cover the sides of the dresser with the fabric. If you see an edge lifting, use some fabric adhesive to hold it in place.

6. Paint the top of the dresser. I did a harlequin design, but you can do something different if you like, such as a polka dot or broad stripe. Just have fun. You can add detail by drawing wavy lines with a gold marker. Outline the harlequin lines (or other design element) with the marker.

7. To add age to the dresser, take a toothbrush dipped in watered-down brown acrylic paint and use your finger to spatter the paint on top of the dresser. Practice this technique on a piece of paper before you attempt it on the dresser. The goal is to achieve a fine mist.

Footstools

We all need a place to put our feet up and relax. Footstools allow us to do just that, while adding a homey feeling and a vintage charm.

I picked up one footstool at a flea market and the other at a second-hand store. You may be surprised at where the top of the yellow oval footstool came from—it's from an old rug that was ruined, except for some small areas. Instead of throwing the rug out, I saved those sections and tossed the rest. Happily, I still have some pieces left over for future projects.

Dena's Tip

Old bits of rug, needlepoint pillows, or other heavy fabrics are excellent covers for footstools. You'll want something sturdy that can take a lot of wear and tear.

Materials

- Wooden footstool
- Fabric adhesive
- Heavy-duty craft scissors
- Newspaper or tracing paper
- Old piece of Oriental or vintage rug
- Permanent marker
- Red buttons
- Tassel trim

Directions

1. Place stool upside down on newspaper and trace the shape of the stool. Make allowances for the width of the top, and add ½" for adhering underneath. Cut out the template.

2. Use the template as a guide to pick a pretty area of the rug. Trace the template onto the bottom of selected area and cut out rug.

3. Apply fabric adhesive to the top of the stool. Place the rug over the adhesive.

4. Cut ½" slits approximately every 2" into the area of the rug that hangs over the stool. Adhere rug to the sides of the stool, then turn the stool over and glue the slitted pieces to the underside of the stool.

5. Glue the trim to the edge of the rug, then glue the buttons on, spacing them evenly around the stool.

Glass Tabletop

This is a great project for a small table or desk with a damaged or unattractive top. This easy project takes about five minutes to assemble. The table can display special invitations, wonderful family photographs, a collage of fabric and pictures, or other mementos from a special occasion. The best part is that you can change it whenever you want.

Dena's Tip

When ordering a glass table-top, be certain to get the edges polished to avoid sharp edges.

Materials

- Table
- Images and fabric as desired
- Piece of glass cut to fit the top of the table
- Scallop-edged scissors

Directions

1. Lay background fabric on the table and arrange images as desired. If using family photos, you may want to trim them with scalloped scissors, then arrange on the table.
2. Place glass over the arrangement.

Wicker Chairs

I bought these wicker chairs from a showroom in San Francisco. When I got them home, I realized I didn't like the way the backs of the chairs looked—they were too plain and not very pretty. Since dining chairs are almost always pulled into the table, chair backs are a key element of the room's decor. The back of the chair should be as interesting and attractive as the front. So I covered each one in a different yet coordinating vintage fabric to make them unique.

Dena's Tip

If you have an item at home that you really don't like or that nees a "facelift" (update), an embellishment project may be just what it needs. Don't be afraid to experiment.

Materials

- Wicker chairs
- Craft scissors
- Fabric adhesive
- Fabric scissors
- Newspaper or tracing paper
- Pencil
- Thin flexible trim to go around the edges of the chair back
- Variety of sturdy coordinating vintage fabrics, enough to cover each chair back plus 1" extra

Directions

1. Make a template with newspaper by outlining the back of the chair exactly where you want to place the fabric.

2. Use the template as a guide to cut the vintage fabric to size and add 1" all around.

3. Fold under the extra inch of fabric and adhere with fabric adhesive to avoid frayed edges. Apply fabric adhesive to the edges of the fabric and adhere to the backs of the chairs.

4. Add a bit more detail and a finished look by adhering thin trim along the glued edges.

Wooden Chairs

I use these chairs at my kitchen table and have started to personalize them. The ones for my daughters Rachel and Lisa have their names on them and a variety of flowers and borders.

I'm working on my son David's chair. It will be more masculine looking, with a picture of his Wheaten Terrier, Daisy. The chairs for David and my husband Dan will have geometric designs on them. I think I will paint a floral design on mine.

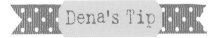

Dena's Tip

When painting chairs that coordinate, I like to use a single color palette. The addition of black and white on the chair adds sophistication and contrast. When I've completed each chair, I add a touch of gold for drama.

Materials

- Wooden chair
- Acrylic paints
- Foam brush
- Gold marker
- Non-yellowing varnish
- Paintbrushes in a variety of sizes
- White gesso

Directions

1. Mix gesso with a small amount of acrylic paint (I used brown and sienna) to create a linen white base coat.

2. Using the foam brush, base-coat the chair with the gesso mixture. Let it dry completely.

3. Lightly sketch a design in pencil onto the chair.

4. Mix paint colors in plastic cups. You can cover unused paint with plastic wrap and a rubber band. You should be able to store the paint for a couple of days.

5. Fill in the sketched design with paint. If you have a chair with a lot of carved details, you can use that detail as a guide for painting. Let dry completely.

6. Use the gold marker for added detail and outline.

7. Finish with a non-yellowing varnish as a protective cover. Each varnish varies, so I recommend following the directions on the can.

Note: I prefer using tinted gesso for my painted furniture. The undercoat should have a flat or eggshell finish. Avoid using glossy paint for the undercoat because it's too slippery to draw on—markers and pencils won't stick.

Tabletop with Pressed Flowers

Here is another great project for hiding an unattractive tabletop. You can do this project with your children. Listen to their ideas and, together, you can create a design that reflects the entire family's tastes.

Dena's Tip

When embellishing a desktop or dresser with drawers, don't forget the knobs. Try gluing stacks of three buttons of different sizes to the tops of flat knobs for a fun and different look.

Materials

- Table or old vanity
- 3 buttons, small, medium, and large, for each knob
- Almond spray paint
- Craft scissors
- Dried pressed flowers
- Flat-topped knobs
- Foam brush
- Glass cut to fit tabletop
- Gold acrylic paint
- Gold ink pad
- Hot-glue gun and glue sticks
- Leaf rubber stamp
- Museum board
- Needle and matching thread
- Paintbrushes in a variety of sizes
- Pencil
- Small piece of coordinating felt
- White craft glue
- White gesso or latex paint

Directions

1. Using a foam brush, paint an old piece of furniture with a base coat of white gesso.

2. To give it a slightly aged look, spray it lightly with almond spray paint.

3. If the tabletop is beyond refinishing, cut a piece of museum board to size.

4. Stamp gold leaves on the museum board.

5. Lay out the dried pressed flowers and secure them in place with a touch of white glue.

6. Place the decorated museum board on the tabletop and place the glass over the board.

7. To give the table a special touch, highlight the carved details by brushing gold paint on them.

8. Hot-glue the small button to the medium button and the medium button to the large button.

9. Trace the large button onto the felt and cut out the felt.

10. Hot-glue the button stack to the felt, then onto the flat-topped knob.

11. Screw the knobs onto the vanity.

♥ Tabletop

At our home, the kitchen and dining-room tables are family gathering spots. It is where we start and end the day together. When we have friends over, we like to start with a warm and inviting table, one that looks like we spent hours making it just right.

Many of the projects in this chapter can be done ahead of time. You can create beautiful placemats, napkins, napkin rings, and coasters, and you can enhance unadorned plates and glasses. Once you finish, you will have a charming table with dinnerware you can use over and again.

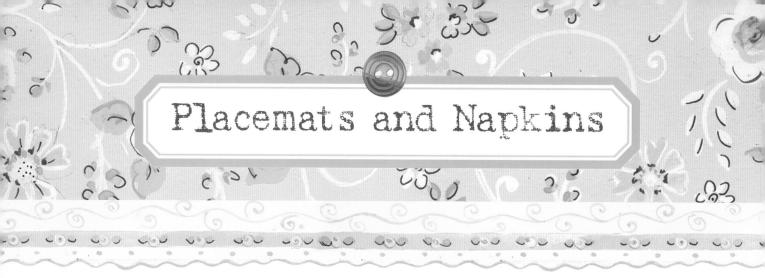

Placemats and Napkins

It's pretty easy to find inexpensive solid-colored placemats and napkins to embellish, and you can choose to do all kinds of different designs, from romantic and vintage to country to modern.

For this project, I created the look of a flowerpot, using pieces from an old chenille bedspread. I also added some painted flowers, but this is optional. The joy of embellishing is choosing how much or how little you want to decorate.

Dena's Tip

Collect beautiful scraps of fabric—quilt pieces, tablecloths, dishtowels, napkins, hankies—and save them for future projects.

Note: Textile medium is an additive that makes paint on fabrics permanent. Simply mix it in equal parts with paint, and it allows the painted fabric to be washable as well as pliable. You can find it at crafts stores.

Materials

- Cloth placemats
- #3 round paintbrush
- Acrylic paints in light and dark green, and light and dark pink
- Chenille fabric
- Coordinating cloth napkins
- Fabric scissors
- Needle and matching thread
- Ribbon flowers, enough for each placemat
- Sewing machine with matching thread
- Textile medium

Directions

1. Cut one flowerpot shape from the chenille fabric for each placemat.

2. Hem the topside of the flowerpots. Fold the remaining edges under and sew them to the left side of the placemat. You will be sewing three sides—not the topside—of the flowerpot to the placemat. That opening will be used for your flatware.

3. Stitch a small ribbon flower to the center of the chenille flowerpot.

4. Using a 1:1 ratio, mix the textile medium with the acrylic paint.

5. Using the #3 round brush, paint some simple flowers on the placemat above your flowerpot.

6. To coordinate the napkins with the placemats, embellish a small corner of each napkin by painting a small flower or vine. Add rickrack trim in a coordinating color, if desired.

Hand-painted Dishes

Some of you may be a little intimidated at the thought of painting. This is a perfect project to get you warmed up to the idea. No master's class in drawing is required here—just straight (or not so straight) lines. We are just using two different-sized brushes to create a plaid pattern, so relax and have fun with this one!

Dena's Tip

If you feel daring, try varying the design of your plaid by experimenting with different brush sizes and coordinating colors.

Note: These plates are mainly for decorative purposes. You don't want to eat off them. You can place paper doilies in the center and serve cookies on them. Your plates will need to be hand-washed. Simply follow the manufacturer's directions on the paint container for drying and permanency.

Materials

- Square white dessert plates
- #5 round paintbrush
- ½" flat paintbrush
- Paper towels
- Art enamels for ceramics and glass in aqua, gold metallic, green, and periwinkle,

Directions

1. Dip the flat paintbrush in water, then wipe off. This will make the brush more pliable. Paint stripes approximately every ½" around the plate border with aqua. Let the paint dry and wash the brush out well.

2. Paint long stripes with green across the stripes.

3. Using the round brush, paint thin stripes in periwinkle on either side of the Green stripe. Let the paint dry and wash the brush out well.

4. Using the round brush, paint small stripes with gold metallic in between stripes of aqua.

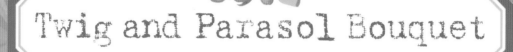

Twig and Parasol Bouquet

This is one of my favorite projects. I adore the combination of the colorful paper parasols, branches from my garden, and "leaves" cut from old books. This arrangement is wonderful during those cold winter months when fresh flowers from the garden are scarce.

Dena's Tip

Paper parasols come in a variety of colors. If you can't find your favorites at your local crafts or party supply store, you can gently spray-paint them with floral spray paint, also available at crafts stores.

Materials

- Branches from your garden
- Decorative-edged scissors
- Heavy-duty craft scissors
- Hot-glue gun and glue sticks
- Pages from an old book or color copies of book pages
- Paper parasols (found at crafts or party supply stores)
- Thin-gauge wire, preferably green
- Vase
- Wire cutters

Directions

1. Arrange branches in vase. Trim them down as necessary, but be sure they have a nice full appearance.
2. Using the decorative-edged scissors, cut leaf shapes from book pages and set aside.
3. Cut the wire into 1½" pieces. Open the parasols and attach them to the branches with wire.
4. Hot-glue the paper leaves to the ends of the twigs.

Silk Flower Dessert Plate with Pedestal

I've been fascinated by miniatures since I was a child. I built dollhouses and designed all the furniture, clothing, and accessories. To me, they were tiny magical environments. This project brings back those wonderful childhood memories and creates a useful and beautiful dessert plate.

I use my cake plate for small cookies and candies. When I make one for a special friend, I add a tiny message that I glue onto the bottom of the goblet or stand.

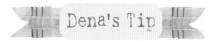

Dena's Tip

Coordinate the flower and decorative paper to go with a favorite dinnerware pattern or dessert plate.

Materials

- Glass dessert plate with a pretty rim
- Footed glass dessert goblet
- #3 round paintbrush
- Clear-drying white craft glue
- Faux pearls
- Glass adhesive
- Green spongy moss
- Large pink silk flower to fit nicely inside dessert goblet
- Pencil
- Pink art enamel for ceramic and glass
- Sheet of coordinating scrapbook paper
- Small piece of coordinating felt
- Small-tipped scissors

Directions

1. Turn the glass plate over and center it on top of the goblet. Paint small pink polka dots around the underside of the plate's rim. Do not paint in central area over goblet. Set the plate aside and let dry.

2. Place green moss in the bottom of the goblet. Place the pink silk flower on top of the moss inside the goblet. Adhere a few pearls inside the center of the silk flower with white glue.

3. Using a pencil, trace around the bottom of the goblet onto pretty scrapbook paper. Cut out the circle with scissors, then cut small slits around the edge of the paper. These slits provide the circle with more give as it is adhered to a surface. They should be approximately ½" deep, cut around the paper edge every 2". Glue paper circle onto the bottom of the goblet with white glue. Smooth out any air bubbles.

4. Repeat Step 3 with the felt. Glue felt over the paper on the bottom of the goblet.

5. Place a small amount of glass adhesive along the top lip of the goblet. Place the glass plate on top of goblet and press down to adhere.

Hand-painted Glasses

I like to paint a variety of designs on a set of glasses so each glass is one-of-a-kind. They shouldn't look like carbon copies of each other. However, it is a good idea to coordinate colors and design themes. This is a great way to design your own set of glasses when you can't find any to go with your dinnerware.

I use these glasses for special occasions since they need to be hand-washed. Friends always ask where I got them—so I know they are noticed!

Dena's Tip

When painting a set of glasses, mix all of your colors first in jars or plastic containers with lids. That way, if you stop and want to continue later, you won't need to remix and match.

Materials

- Glasses
- #2 or #3 round paintbrush
- Art enamels for ceramics and glass in a variety of colors

Directions

1. Paint glasses with any design you like and let them dry according to paint manufacturer's directions.
2. If desired, add a touch of black, like a tiny polka dot around the base or an accent stripe elsewhere.

Coasters

I like making these coasters as gifts. When giving them to someone, you won't need to cover them with gift paper—they are pretty on their own. Just stack them and tie with a pretty length of ribbon.

The pressed flowers in the coasters look pretty and you can buy them at a crafts store or better yet, press your own flowers from your garden.

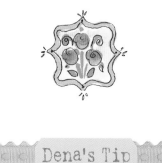

Dena's Tip

For a variation, try different background papers adhered to museum board. Using copies of your favorite poems or jokes would make for a great conversation piece.

Materials

- Thin squares of cork
- 2 butterfly or bull-nose clips
- Floral or leaf rubber stamp
- Glass squares, cut to size of cork squares
- Gold ink pad
- Metallic gold tape
- Museum board, cut to size of cork squares
- Pressed flowers
- Small foam brush
- White craft glue

Directions

1. Stamp a simple design on the museum board, using the floral stamp and gold ink pad.

2. Arrange pressed flowers in a pleasing design on top of the museum board, then glue them down.

3. Sandwich the cork, museum board, and glass together. Clip on two sides with butterfly clips. This will hold all of the materials in place as you tape all four sides with the metallic gold tape. Try to keep the tape even and straight. Remove the butterfly clips as you finish taping each side.

Note: Thin squares of cork are usually sold as plain coasters in home stores, and you can find metallic gold tape at crafts stores.

Napkin Rings

I think of napkin rings as jewelry for my table. The napkin ring you choose to embellish should fit nicely with the trim or ribbon you've chosen. If you want the edges of the napkin ring to show, choose a slightly smaller ribbon. If not, find a ribbon exactly the same width. It's helpful to bring the napkin ring along to make sure the ribbon is not wider than the napkin ring.

Depending on how you want to set your table, you can choose elegant or casual trims and ribbons for this project.

Materials

- Napkin rings
- Fabric adhesive
- Grosgrain ribbon
- Hot-glue gun and glue sticks
- Small-tipped scissors
- Vintage silver button or other buttons

Directions

1. Tie grosgrain ribbon in a small bow. Sew a button to the center of the bow.
2. Using fabric adhesive, glue another length of grosgrain ribbon around the napkin ring, then hot-glue the bow with the button onto the napkin ring.

Dena's Tip

Start saving miniature embellishments for this project. Small buttons, charms, paper or felt flowers, seashells, and bits of vintage jewelry all work well for this project.

Bowl of Lemons

Embellishing doesn't get easier than this project. When you don't have time to put together an elaborate floral arrangement, a simple bowl of lemons (or other fruit) with the addition of moss is absolutely beautiful in its simplicity.

I like to keep a variety of bowls in different patterns and colors on hand. Since I like vintage dinnerware, I usually purchase bowls at flea markets. Keep a bag of moss in your crafts closet—it comes in handy for so many projects.

Dena's Tip

Don't skimp on the fruit in your bowl. More is better in this case.

Materials

- Pretty bowl
- Fresh lemons
- Moss

Directions

1. Arrange a bed of moss in the bowl and add lemons. Make sure the bowl is nice and full. Add more moss around the lemons until you achieve the desired look.

Lighting and Candles

While we all know that the right lighting is crucial to creating a mood in a room, how often do we overlook the light fixtures themselves? Lampshades and their bases are like blank canvases waiting for your creative touch. Using beads, fabric, and various trims, you can transform light fixtures into usable artworks.

While you are at it, remember candlelight. Softly glowing votives and elegant tapers on a dinner table or mantel evoke feelings of romance and warmth, even more so when they're presented in embellished holders.

Candelabra Embellished with Moss, Vines, and Flowers

I bought this candelabra at a garage sale years ago. I never truly loved it—it was a bit nondescript—but I liked the shape, it was functional, and it was cheap! I did see the potential for something special eventually. I knew it would look great with the tiny vines called smilax that I grow in my garden. These vines are also available at nurseries. They are easy to twist and knot for this and many other projects.

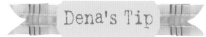

Dena's Tip

Buy old millinery flower hats at tag sales, flea markets, and thrift shops. If they are a bit tired looking, so much the better.

Materials

- Candelabra or chandelier fixture
- Chandelier crystals with wire
- Feather butterfly, small bee, or dragonfly
- Floral moss
- Hot-glue gun and glue sticks
- Wire vine
- Vintage millinery flowers

Directions

1. Place moss around the fixture and hot-glue into place.
2. Gently twine the smilax around the fixture and attach with wire.
3. Add wire crystal around the base of each candle.
4. Hot-glue millinery flowers as desired.
5. Hot-glue the feather insect onto a millinery flower for an added whimsical touch.

Fabric Lampshade with Embellishments

I always have fun sorting through my piles of fabric, looking for just the right one for the project I'm working on at the moment. Each fabric brings back memories of my treasure-hunting adventures.

While sorting through fabrics at one of my favorite fabric stores, this unusual sculpted tulle caught my eye. I purchased about ½ yard. At the time, I didn't know what I would use it for, so it went into my crafts closet until I thought of it for this project.

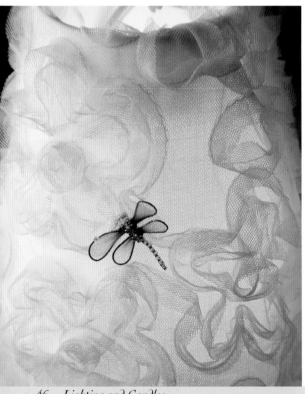

Dena's Tip

A feather butterfly, dragonfly, or a tiny bird adds a bit of whimsy to a project. It makes you smile each time you see it.

Materials

- Lampshade and base
- Cream-colored paper flowers
- Embellished sheer fabric, enough to fit around a lampshade plus a bit extra to tuck under
- Fabric scissors
- Fabric-marking pen
- Hot-glue gun and glue sticks

Directions

1. Lay fabric out on a flat surface and place the shade on top of it.
2. Using the fabric-marking pen, trace the shade by rolling it over the fabric in a complete circle. Include an extra 1" as you trace both the top edge and bottom edge.
3. Cut the fabric and carefully hot-glue it to the lampshade. Tuck raw edges under and hot-glue to the inside of the shade.
4. Hot-glue a border of pretty paper flowers around the base of the shade.

Ribbon Lamp with Embellished Shade

The majority of lampshades are either beige or white. Others have specific designs. While many are attractive, they just might not fit in with your home's decor. Personally, I like the neutral surfaces because the decorating possibilities are endless.

You can embellish, using paints, stamps, markers, jewels, fabrics, and more. For this lamp, I used two different ribbons on the base: a wired ribbon that's easy to wrap in concentric circles around the base, and a pretty green velvet ribbon on the top section. For the shade, I used acrylic paints, faux pearls, and a custom border.

Dena's Tip

If a lampshade is too short and shows the hardware or even the bottom of the bulb, cut a band from artist's canvas or glue pretty paper to museum board, then scallop the edge and adhere the strip to the inside edge of your shade to make it longer.

Materials

For Lamp base

- 1" wide velvet ribbon, enough to wrap around upper half of the lamp pole
- 1" wide or narrower wire-edged ribbon enough to wrap around the entire base of the lamp and up the pole

- Simple wooden lamp base
- Craft scissors
- Fabric adhesive
- Heavy-duty double-sided tape
- Hot-glue gun and glue sticks
- Velvet millinery flower

Directions

1. Begin with the wire-edged ribbon. Tuck under the raw edge and secure with fabric adhesive. Using double-sided tape, adhere to the lamp base, slowly winding the ribbon around the entire base and halfway up the pole. If the base is round, you will want to wrap the ribbon in concentric circles.

2. Switch to velvet ribbon once you get halfway up the pole. Secure with double-sided tape and a bit of adhesive at the end.

3. Hot-glue a millinery flower at the point where the ribbons switch.

Materials

For Lampshade:

- Plain cream or white fabric lampshade
- 1" foam brush
- 2"-wide piece of canvas
- Acrylic paints in lavender and white
- Craft scissors
- Faux pearls
- Hot-glue gun and glue sticks
- Pen
- Water
- White gesso

Directions

1. Paint the canvas strip with gesso. Let it dry completely.

2. Water down lavender paint to the consistency of cream. Using the foam brush, paint the shade. Let it dry.

3. Paint small white flowers onto the shade. Let it dry.

4. Paint a lavender stripe freehand onto the canvas strip. Let it dry.

5. Hot-glue faux pearls onto the centers of flowers.

6. Draw scallops along one side of the canvas strip. You can use a circle template to draw the scallops. Cut alongside the scalloped pen marks so that the pen lines don't show.

7. Hot-glue the scalloped border to the inside of the base of the shade, making sure ½"–¾" of the border shows.

Stamped and Beaded Lampshade

Stamping is great for so many projects. I like using gold ink; it adds a certain amount of elegance to finished products such as this classic lampshade.

I was thrilled to be able to use the lovely glass charms I've collected over the years on this project. I'm sure those special jewels you have tucked away in a dresser drawer will soon be on display in a new treasure you have created.

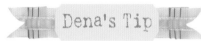 **Dena's Tip**

Don't throw away those old broken necklaces—they make great embellishments.

Materials

- Lampshade
- Almond spray paint
- Beads
- Earring wires
- Gold ink pad
- Needle-nosed pliers
- Rubber stamp
- Scrapbooking awl or large needle
- Wire cutters

Directions

1. Spray lampshade with almond spray paint to give it an aged look. Let paint dry.
2. Stamp the lampshade with the rubber stamp and gold ink in an allover pattern.
3. Pierce holes around the base of the lampshade with a scrapbooking awl. Be careful of your fingers as you make the holes.
4. Thread beads on the earring wire. Attach wires to the lampshade and bend them with pliers to secure.
5. Trim the wires.

Basket Lamp

This project is great because there are so many possibilities. You can go simple with moss and apples and some fresh ivy or let your imagination run wild to create a wonderful environment, using some miniature figurines, tiny flowers, and other objects that are waiting for a home. Just look in your crafts treasure chest and around your home.

The great thing about this lamp is that you can change it on a whim. The basket and fixture stay the same but the scene or contents can change from season to season or holiday to holiday.

Materials

- Vintage wicker basket with handle
- Chandelier crystals with wire
- Clamp-on basket-adapter lamp socket
- Floral moss
- Foam oasis
- Hot-glue gun and glue sticks
- Miniature ceramic animals or figures
- Paper flowers
- Scissors
- Twig from your garden
- Vines from your garden
- Vintage ephemera
- Wire
- Wire cutters

Directions

1. Fill the bottom of the basket with oasis. Cover the oasis with moss.

2. Wrap the wire from the basket adapter lamp around the basket handle and screw the basket-adapter lamp hardware in place at the center of the handle.

3. Cover the basket's handle with vine, using wire to secure in place.

4. Wire small leaves around a twig to make it look like a small tree.

5. Hot-glue small decorative elements in place to create a vignette. (I used a couple of ceramic dogs, glued a small tea set to a piece of fabric, then placed paper flowers around.)

6. Attach crystals to the handle with wire.

Dena's Tip

If you can't find a basket lamp fixture in a hardware store, search the Internet under "lamp fixtures."

Hand-painted Chinese Lantern

When I saw these sheer fabric lanterns in a variety of pastel colors in a gift shop, I was enamored. These would be lovely hanging in my studio; but they had to be painted and embellished, of course. I was amazed at how easily the sheer fabric held the paint. I used gouache paint, which is an opaque watercolor. The colors are lovely and can be painted over, unlike regular watercolors.

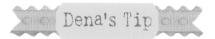
Dena's Tip

When painting objects, use the natural framework to dictate placement of your design. For example, on the lantern, I let the wire frame along the top and bottom be my guide for adding the scalloped border.

Materials

- Fabric Chinese lanterns
- Fabric tassel
- Gouache paints in green, pink, red, and white
- Iridescent gold acrylic paint
- Paintbrushes in a variety of sizes
- Palette
- Paper flowers
- Small chain, as long as necessary for where lantern will hang
- Small foam brush
- Thin-gauge wire

Directions

1. Paint the wood at the top and bottom of the lantern, using a foam brush and the iridescent gold paint.

2. Draw a scallop with the green paint around the top edge and bottom edge of the lantern, then go back and fill in with paint.

3. To make the roses, make a slightly scalloped circle with white paint, then go back and add some light pink and then red in the center. Paint three roses on each side of the lantern. Paint leaves with the roses and add little branches with leaves.

4. To camouflage the chain, attach paper flowers to it with wire.

5. Attach the chain with a small piece of wire to the loop at the top of the lantern.

6. Add the fabric tassel at the bottom of the lantern.

Chandelier with Embellished Shades

This white wrought-iron chandelier with yellow roses has been in my house for years. While I love it, I was ready for a change. So to freshen it up, I decided to add some small shades that I embellished with paint and tassel trims. Now, I feel as though I have a new chandelier.

Materials

- Small light-colored paper lamp-shades to fit chandelier
- #2 round paintbrush
- Acrylic paints in gold and soft buttery yellow
- Hot-glue gun and glue sticks
- Plastic disposable cup
- Small damp kitchen sponge
- Tassel trim, enough to go around the base of all shades
- Water

Dena's Tip

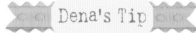

Bring your shades with you to the trim store and try multiple styles. You might want to layer trims for a unique and detailed design.

Directions

1. In a plastic cup, mix yellow acrylic paint with water until it has a creamy consistency. Dip the damp kitchen sponge into the paint and sponge the paint onto the shades. Just a little paint is necessary. Let the paint dry to the touch.

2. Using the round brush and gold acrylic paint, paint a wavy line all the way around the base. Add gold polka dots or small gold leaves inside each scallop, if desired.

3. Hot-glue tassel trim around the base of each shade.

Decoupage Votives

What makes these votives so special is the combination of decorative tissue paper or fiber and vintage clipart icons. Try adding a bit of glitter for extra "glam."

I like using these at dinner parties. It's nice to make a small one to place in front of each place setting. Your guests can take them home as party favors.

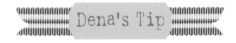

Dena's Tip

Gold markers also come in 14-karat gold. This is great for the top edge of your glass or other craft project.

Materials

- Juice glass with smooth sides
- 1 foam brush
- Craft scissors
- Decoupage medium
- Metallic gold marker with a broad tip
- Paper towels
- Pen
- Transparent decorative paper or fiber
- Vintage image

Directions

1. Lay two paper towels on a flat surface. Place the juice glass on its side and slowly roll it across the paper towels while tracing the glass to make a template.
2. Place template on transparent paper or fiber. Cut to fit, adding ½" for the seam allowance.
3. Using a foam brush and decoupage medium, adhere paper to the outside of juice glass. Let it dry.
4. Trim the paper edges on the top and bottom.
5. Using decoupage medium, adhere vintage image over decorative paper.
6. Using the marker, add a band of gold onto the lip of the glass for a finished look.

Beaded Candle

This project takes only a few minutes to complete, so you can make a lot of them in one sitting. Just make sure the beads you use are not too large, as they will be harder to stick to the candle.

These also make great hostess gifts. Simply tie a beautiful ribbon around a pair and add a gift tag. Also, note that these are quite useable; but make sure to blow them out before the flame gets to the beaded section.

Dena's Tip

Blue painter's tape works great in a project like this. It keeps your glue and beads right where you want them.

Materials

- Taper candles in a variety of heights
- Blue painter's tape
- Small glass beads
- Waxed paper
- White tacky glue

Directions

1. Adhere a strip of blue painter's tape approximately 2" up from the bottom of the candle. Leave a 1" space and adhere a second strip of painter's tape.
2. Apply tacky glue between strips of tape.
3. Place beads on waxed paper. Roll candle on beads. Let beads dry in place and remove painter's tape.

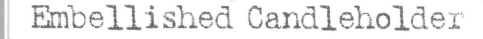

Embellished Candleholder

As much as I love crafting, I enjoy it more when I share it with friends. This candleholder was created with friends during one of our craft weekends. Six of us get together, teach each other new projects, enjoy wonderful food, and stay up till the wee hours of the morning, creating, laughing, and having the best time. This was one of our group projects that I thought you might enjoy, too. It's a delightful project to make at a crafts party of your own.

Materials

- Glass candleholder with smooth surface and interesting shape
- Craft scissors
- Hot-glue gun and glue sticks
- Variety of embellishments including small mother-of-pearl buttons, tassel trim, other trims in a variety of widths, and paper ephemera
- White craft glue

Directions

1. Adhere a variety of embellishments onto the candleholder with glue. Use hot-glue for heavier, bulkier items and white glue for lighter items.

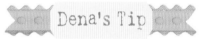

Dena's Tip

Try making these candleholders in odd numbers—3 or 5—and in different heights. They look great grouped on a table.

Gifts

Personalizing gifts adds value to the present. The extra time and thought that goes into the gift shows someone how much you really care. These gifts are practical, pretty, and perfect for giving to a truly special friend, coworker, teacher, or acquaintance. Even the person who has everything and can be difficult to shop for will appreciate the time and effort you put into handcrafting something special for them.

From a simple wrapped bar of soap to a more elaborate breakfast tray or a "feel better" hot-water bottle, the recipients of these one-of-a-kind gifts will immediately know how much you love them.

Breakfast Tray

I have a stack of drawings and paintings that my children have created over the years. It's impossible to hang all of them. This breakfast tray is a great project for showcasing one of those drawings. My collection of old buttons also comes in handy for this project. I'll find any excuse to use this tray.

Materials

- Child's artwork color-copied to fit size of frame
- 1" foam brushes
- 11" x 14" black picture frame with glass and cardboard backing
- Black acrylic paint
- Drawer pulls with hardware
- Flat-head screwdriver
- Gem adhesive
- Glazing points
- Philips screwdriver
- Power drill
- Small disposable dish for holding glue
- Tiny faux-pearl beads
- Tweezers
- Vintage and new buttons

Dena's Tip

You can create a collage by combining the drawing with special notes your children wrote to you, and perhaps a treasured photograph. I'm sure your children, like ours, will be proud to have these things displayed so beautifully.

Directions

1. Paint the underside of the picture frame with the black acrylic paint, using a foam brush. The back side of the frame will actually become the top of the breakfast tray. The small lip around the inside edge of the frame will hold the weight of the glass and picture.

2. Drill holes on both ends of the frame for drawer pulls.

3. Attach drawer pulls with a screwdriver. Make sure the screws are not longer than the width of the frame or they will stick out. A good hardware store will have the proper size screws.

4. Place some gem adhesive in a small dish. Starting with the larger buttons, brush gem adhesive on the bottom of the buttons and adhere to the underside of the painted frame. Continue gluing in the corners and evenly around the tray border, fitting in the smaller sizes as you go.

5. Pick up tiny pearl beads with tweezers and dip them into gem adhesive. Use the beads to fill in the empty spaces of the frame.

6. Lay the cardboard frame backing on the bottom of the frame, then lay the artwork on top of the backing.

7. Place glass on top and finish by inserting glazing points into the wood frame to secure the glass. Gently press on the glazing points with a flat screwdriver.

Albums and Journals

Inexpensive albums and journals are usually easy to come by, especially if the covers aren't too attractive. Don't shy away from these—buy a bunch for future gifts. All they need is a fresh face; and with embellishing, we've got it covered!

Dena's Tip

Small scraps of beautiful fabric should be saved for this project. Even a beautifully embroidered vintage napkin can cover a small notebook.

Materials

- Album or journal
- Fabric adhesive
- Fabric scissors
- Fabric scraps, larger than album or journal by 1" all around
- Flat craft stick
- Spray adhesive
- Variety of embellishments including glitter, three-dimensional items, etc.

Directions

1. Outside or in a well-ventilated area, spray a heavy coat of spray adhesive on wrong side of fabric.
2. Adhere fabric to album, leaving 1" all around. Be sure to smooth out any air bubbles. Cut off the corners of the fabric, leaving $\frac{1}{8}$" of fabric from the corner of the album.
3. At both sides of the album's spine, cut two small flaps to tuck inside the spine.
4. Use craft stick to apply fabric adhesive to excess fabric. Fold the excess fabric inside the book. Fold in and glue fabric to the front and back of the book.
5. Using spray adhesive, adhere the front and back pages of the album to the inside front and back covers.
6. Have fun adding embellishments. Experiment with embellishments to make each album different.

Wrapped Soap

You know the scenario: you go into a boutique and see a beautifully wrapped bar of soap, but the price is exorbitant. You can wrap it much more beautifully yourself for a fraction of the price (gift tag included). So let's do it! I'm sure you have a favorite bar of soap with a lovely scent. Buy it plain and simple and I'll show you how to give it some style.

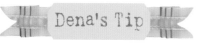
Dena's Tip

When designing packaging such as this, stay with a theme. For example, for this sea theme, you can add some sea glass.

Materials

- Fragrant soap
- Coordinating ribbon or silky seam binding
- Fabric scissors
- Faux pearls
- Hot-glue gun and glue sticks
- Pastel-colored tulle
- Permanent marker
- Variety of small shells

Directions

1. Place the soap on the tulle and cut a square large enough to bunch up around the soap.

2. Place the soap in the center of the tulle square along with a few shells and faux pearls.

3. Gather up each corner of the tulle and secure with seam binding or ribbon, tying a bow.

4. Choose a shell with a surface smooth enough to write on and hot-glue a pearl to the inside. Write a short message around the shell with permanent marker.

5. Hot-glue the shell onto one end of the seam binding or ribbon.

Scottie Dog Shaped Hot-water Bottle Cover

When I was a child I had a basic red hot-water bottle that I used whenever I was under the weather. Now my children have one; and since I am known as the person who loves to embellish, I thought this project would bring a smile to them when they really need it. My kids love this hot-water bottle so much that they ask for it even when they are not sick. It's like having a warm stuffed animal in bed.

Materials

- Red hot-water bottle
- 1 yard fleece or other fuzzy fabric
- Buttons, 2 large white and 2 small black
- Craft scissors
- Cutting mat
- Fabric scissors
- Needle and matching thread
- Pinking shears
- Polyester batting
- Scrap of fleece for hankie collar
- Sewing machine and matching thread
- Straight pins
- Tailor's chalk
- Template

Directions

1. Photocopy Scottie Dog Pattern, enlarging by 300%.

2. Using craft scissors, cut out template pieces. Pin in place on back side of fabric, making sure the two pieces meet. Trace with tailor's chalk and cut out in one piece with fabric scissors. This will be the front of the dog.

3. Turn the template pieces over so they are facing the opposite direction. Give each template piece extra room on the fabric. Trace one template, then shift it over 1" so that you are adding an extra 1" to the dog's belly. Trace the line again. Do the same with the other template piece. This will create a larger seam allowance for the opening. Cut the two pieces out.

4. Hem the belly side of each back piece. Pin the two back pieces to the front piece. Make sure the fuzzy side of the fleece is on the inside.

5. Sew around the outer edges. If fabric is stiff, you may need to take scissors and snip around the corners. This will give fabric some give and it will avoid pull marks. Turn the dog inside out.

6. Place the larger white button on the bottom and the black button on top for the pupil. Stitch on buttons for eyes.

7. Stuff dog head with polyester batting.

8. Cut doggie scarf from fleece in a triangular shape and tie around neck.

9. Insert water bottle into opening.

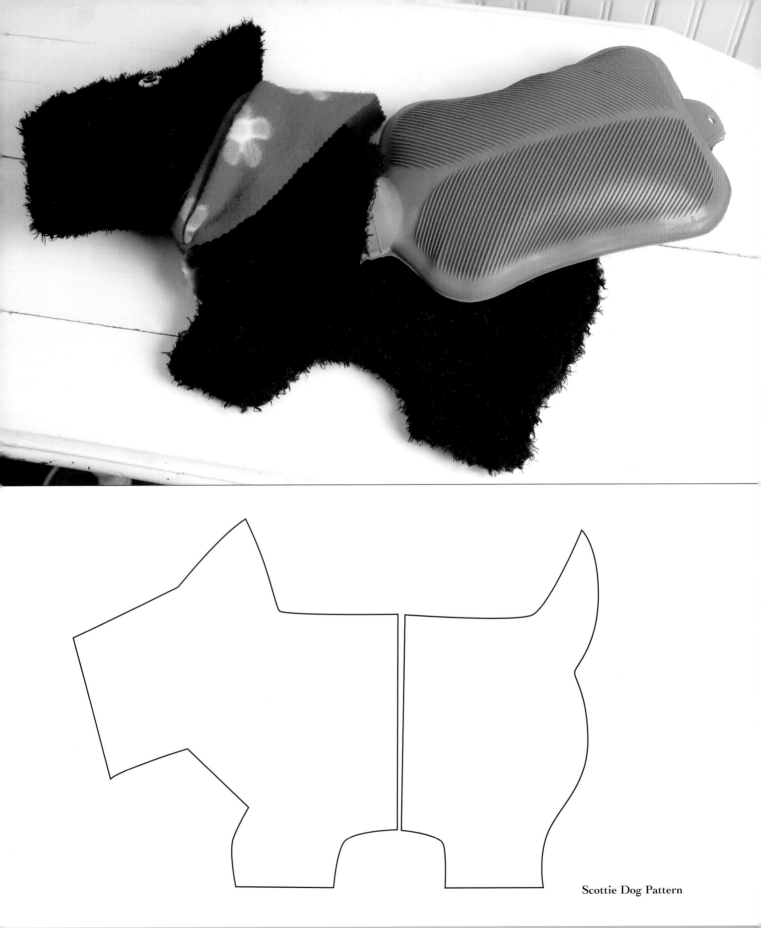

Scottie Dog Pattern

Sachet Pillows from Vintage Hankies and Napkins

Don't you just love the patterns on vintage hankies and napkins? Maybe you once had a gorgeous set of embroidered napkins, but over the years your set has dwindled due to staining or loss. If you have a few left, that's great. We'll put them to good use and you'll love the result.

Dena's Tip

If you can only muster up one hankie or napkin, simply use a coordinated cotton fabric as the back.

Note: If you have napkins that have a fringe, you can sew the napkins together, tie a ribbon around the pillow and tuck flowers in the center.

Materials

- Vintage napkin or hankie
- 2 coordinating buttons in different sizes
- Bag of buckwheat hulls
- Bag of dried lavender
- Coordinating trim
- Fabric adhesive
- Fabric scissors
- Funnel
- Large bowl
- Measuring cups
- Needle and matching thread
- Sewing machine and thread

Directions

1. Fold up a napkin one-third of the way to look like a purse. Sew seams on each side. The remaining fabric will become the top "flap" of the "purse."

2. Fold the top flap over and sew the folded area together, leaving a 3" opening on one end.

3. Mix two parts buckwheat hulls to one part dried lavender in a large bowl and set aside.

4. Fill the pillow with the buckwheat and lavender mixture by pouring it through the funnel from a measuring cup.

5. Sew the pillow closed.

6. Glue the trim onto the top flap's edge with fabric adhesive, leaving 1" on each end so that you can tuck it under. Let the glue dry.

7. Working with the buttons, place the smaller button on top of the larger button and stitch both onto the center of the flap over the trim. If desired, tack the corner flaps down.

Embellished Photo Frame Mat Boards

Photo frame mat boards are inexpensive, fun to decorate, and the flat surface makes it easy to apply embellishments. I like to add a ribbon hanger on the back of the board. Since the board is lightweight, it hangs nicely and the ribbon stays in place.

This is a fun project to do with family or friends. Your friends can bring a variety of materials to share—and some snacks. You can turn on some fun background music for a creative day of togetherness and embellishing.

Materials

- Photo frame mat board
- Coordinating scrapbook papers in 2 or 3 designs
- Coordinating trims and ribbons
- Craft knife
- Cutting mat
- Double-sided tape
- Spray adhesive
- Variety of embellishments including stickers, pop dots, glitter, buttons, and vintage jewelry
- White tacky glue

Dena's Tip

When using certain glues and spray adhesives, make sure you are outside or in a well-ventilated area.

Directions

1. Arrange the scrapbook papers in a pleasing pattern and adhere them with spray adhesive to the mat board.

2. On cutting mat, turn mat board over and use craft knife to cut an X from corner to corner of the board's opening. Fold paper back, adhering excess to the back of the board.

3. Have fun adding trims, buttons, glitter, and other gems with white tacky glue.

Mirror Tray for Perfume Bottles

Old perfume bottles are so pretty to display, and a mirror is a great way to showcase them. Finding a mirrored tray to suit your style can be a bit difficult, though; so here is a project that allows you to design your own tray using trims of your choice. It's extra nice if you can find a beveled mirror. The shape is up to you—anything will work.

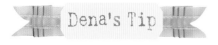

Dena's Tip

Try finding trim that is flexible if you have a mirror with curves. Trim with a scalloped edge is more interesting on the surface and more forgiving on corners and curves.

Materials

- Round mirror with beveled edge
- 4 unfinished wooden drawer pulls
- Art enamels for ceramics and glass in engine red, evergreen, fresh foliage, frost white, gold, and rose shimmer
- Fabric adhesive
- Gold acrylic paint
- Hot-glue gun and glue sticks
- Plastic disposable cup
- Sturdy cardboard, cut 1" larger all around than the mirror
- Tulle with mini rose trim or other pretty flexible trim to go around edge of mirror
- Variety of paintbrushes
- Velvet fabric

Directions

1. In a plastic cup, mix the rose shimmer and white paints to get a pink hue. All other colors are used straight from the bottle.
2. Use a detail brush to paint a vine and rosebuds onto the mirror's edge. Let paint dry.
3. Paint the drawer pulls with gold acrylic paint. Set aside to dry.
4. Apply fabric adhesive to the cardboard and glue velvet onto cardboard. Press down. Apply fabric adhesive to the raw edges of velvet and wrap onto bottom side of cardboard. Pleat the fabric as necessary.
5. Using fabric adhesive, glue the mirror to the fabric-covered cardboard.
6. Hot-glue the painted drawer pulls to the bottom of the cardboard.
7. Using fabric adhesive, glue the tulle and mini rose trim around the edges of the mirror.

Accessories

It always amazes me how much I am drawn to details in a home. Carefully considered accessories catch the eye and add a one-of-a-kind, special touch. For example, the turquoise and chocolate-colored switch plates in this chapter are in a hallway in my house. It makes a playful, attractive design statement in an otherwise boring space.

Small accessories can pull a room together and dress it up in a variety of styles, from vintage to thoroughly modern. What's more, accessories and embellishing go hand-in-hand. Accessories like plain picture frames, salt and pepper shakers, and solid-colored throw pillows are the perfect blank canvases for embellishments.

Speaking of embellishing, I think I now have to paint my hallway to go with my pretty switch plates. Shouldn't that have been the other way around? Hmmm…

Yellow Rose Curtain Tiebacks

This project takes a bit more time than the others in this book and it is truly well worth the effort. To start, choose a fabric that goes well with your room's decor. I chose yellow cotton velvet because it's an accent color in my dining room. You will need sturdy curtain backs as your base to sew the roses onto.

What I like about this project is that there is no "right way" to fabricate a flower. Each one will be a little different. The roses should look like they're in different stages of bloom—some smaller, others larger. Make a lot of roses and leaves first, then piece them together like a puzzle onto the tiebacks.

Dena's Tip

I like to sew while watching TV. I keep a basket full of supplies for the project I'm working on by my bedside. By having it all in one place, you are more likely to pick it up and work on it.

Materials

- Premade fabric curtain tiebacks
- Cotton velvets in green and yellow
- Fabric scissors
- Needle and matching thread
- Straight pins
- Thin-gauge wire
- Wire cutters

Directions

1. To form a rose, cut a length of yellow velvet approximately 5" x 24". Vary the width and length of the roses to get a variety of sizes.

2. Tucking the short end in, begin by tightly twisting the velvet and rolling it into a spiral. As you roll, stitch the spiral together underneath. When you come to the end of the flower, tuck the end under and stitch down. Try to get a fairly flat base on most of the flowers.

3. Stitch flowers to curtain tiebacks.

4. For the leaves, cut the green fabric in varied leaf shapes and sizes. Stitch right sides together and leave an opening at the bottom of each leaf.

5. Bend wire into a leaf shape and insert through the bottom of each leaf. Stitch the leaves onto the curtain tieback between the roses.

6. Bend the wired leaves into natural leaf shapes.

Vintage Bulletin Board and Decorative Tacks

This project turns a plain bulletin board into a work of art. Basically, you are covering foam-core board or a bulletin board with lovely fabric, then attaching it to a pretty frame. Easy? You bet! That gives you more time to create some fabulous tacks for your board. I've seen these in stores and they are so expensive. Plus, yours will be so much cuter.

Dena's Tip

Tacks such as these can be used in a variety of ways. You can use decorative tacks to add a wonderful detail to shelf-edging paper or to hang small photos on walls.

Materials

For bulletin board:

◆ Old picture frame
◆ ¼"-thick foam-core board
◆ Fabric adhesive
◆ Fabric scissors
◆ Heavy-duty tape, such as duct tape
◆ Sturdy fabric to fit on foam-core board plus 1" all around

Directions

1. Apply fabric adhesive to wrong side of fabric in a well-ventilated area.
2. Place fabric onto the board and fold edges under. If necessary, add a bit of fabric adhesive to edges.
3. Using duct tape, attach fabric-covered board to back of frame.

Materials

For decorative tacks:

◆ Flat-topped upholstery tacks
◆ Hot-glue gun and glue sticks
◆ Variety of embellishments including fabric or felt flowers, buttons, bits of old earrings, small shells, rhinestones, and watch faces

Directions

1. Hot-glue small embellishments onto tacks.

Layered Decorative Pillows

In this project, I used inexpensive plain throw pillows so I didn't have to start completely from scratch. The pillows were neutral and were in desperate need of embellishing. Adding three-dimensional elements turned them into charming accents for the home.

Materials

- Solid-color foam-filled throw pillows
- Fabric adhesive
- Fabric scissors
- Needle and matching thread
- Three-dimensional embellishments including buttons, rhinestones, and bows
- Variety of trims
- Vintage bits of fabric, including needlepoint, embroidered napkins, or tea towels

Dena's Tip

Instead of using foam, you can substitute down for a more luxurious feel.

Directions

1. Layer bits of vintage fabric onto the front of the pillow to set the design. Stitch the fabric to the pillow.

2. Using fabric adhesive or a needle and thread, attach trim to the face of the pillow. Stitch or glue embellishments as desired to different areas of the vintage fabrics. (For example, I stitched a ribbon to the dog's collar on the needlepoint fabric.)

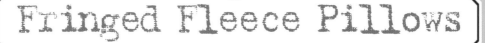

Fringed Fleece Pillows

A friend showed me how to make this project and I was so excited that I went home and made four more pillows right away. The basic pillow-making part of this project is easy and your embellishments can be as simple or as complex as you like. It's totally up to you.

Dena's Tip

It's nice to use two colors of fleece for this pillow project so that you will have two-toned fringe.

Materials

- Foam pillow form
- 2 pieces coordinating fleece cut to pillow size, plus 2½" all around
- Needle and matching thread
- Pinking shears
- Small pieces of fleece in a variety of colors and sizes for embellishments
- Variety of three-dimensional embellishments

Directions

1. Lay two pieces of fleece on a flat surface, one on top of the other, with the edges perfectly aligned.

2. Lay the pillow form in the center so fleece extends 2½" on all sides.

3. With pinking shears, cut 2½" squares from both pieces of fleece at each corner. Cut strips 2½" long and ½" wide all the way around the pillow on both pieces of fleece.

4. Tie the upper and lower strips of the fleece together in double knots. Continue tying on three sides. Slip in pillow form, then finish knotting the fourth side.

5. Embellish the face of the pillow as desired.

Newspaper Shelf Edging

I still don't understand why manufacturers don't come out with a great line of shelf-edging paper. The look was once so popular in the 1950s—and for good reason: it's absolutely charming. So until this product is out in the market, we can have a great time making our own.

I like using the classified section for this project because the words are close together and there are no photos.

Dena's Tip

For extra detail, add embellished tacks from the Vintage Bulletin Board and decorative Tacks project on page 84. You can also add pieces of jewelry, decorative papers, pompom trims, beaded trims, and other embellishments.

Materials

- Newspaper
- Craft scissors
- Double-sided tape
- Flat-back buttons
- Glossy wood-tone spray finish
- Hole punch
- Hot-glue gun and glue sticks
- Pushpins or upholstery tacks

Directions

1. Using spray finish, lightly spray classified section for a vintage look. Let dry, then cut the newspaper into approximately 2"-wide strips.

2. Cut a zigzag pattern along one edge of the strips.

3. Using one or a variety of hole punches, punch a pattern along the zigzag edge.

4. Attach to shelf edge with double-sided tape.

5. Hot-glue buttons to tops of pushpins or upholstery tacks.

6. Attach button pushpins every 4"–6".

Simple Pillow Slipcover

If you want an easy and beautiful project, then this is for you. This is one of those instant-gratification projects that you can't help but love. I actually used an old table runner for my pillow slipcover. The edges were already finished, so I just had to run a seam up the back.

For this project, part of the pillow will show, so choose a pretty pillow that coordinates with your fabric.

Dena's Tip

Don't throw a perfectly good pillow away because you're tired of it or it's bland. This project will give it new life.

Materials

- Pillow with a nice fabric cover
- Fabric, cut to pillow size plus 1" all around
- Fabric scissors
- Millinery flower
- Needle and matching thread
- Sewing machine and matching thread
- Wide velvet ribbon, enough to tie around center, plus bow
- Variety of embellishments including bows, fabric flowers, etc.

Directions

1. Cut a strip of fabric to fit around pillow. Hem the sides. Sew a seam along the back to make a tube and place it over the pillow.

2. Tie a knot around the pillow with the velvet ribbon. Make a fairly big bow with velvet ribbon and stitch edges together.

3. Stitch the millinery flower to center of bow.

Memory Shadowboxes

This is a charming way to document a recent vacation or special event in your life. I'm sure you have small ephemera such as ticket stubs, invitations, and photos from travel brochures put away somewhere. Bring them out of the drawer and put them on display in a small shadow box with special embellishments.

Be prepared—this project will stir up a flood of fond memories!

Note: You can make a sign by writing your destination and gluing it to the background or by mounting the sign to a piece of string, then attaching the string to the ceiling of the shadowbox. Be sure not to cover this with other embellishments.

Another cheerful option is to make an awning by gluing the paper to heavier cardstock. Scallop the edges with scissors, then hot-glue to the outside of your shadowbox.

Dena's Tip

Start with a smaller shadowbox for this project. I find that working on a small scale with something like this is much less intimidating.

Materials

- Shadowbox
- Buttons
- Craft knife
- Craft scissors
- Cutting mat
- Decorative scrapbook papers
- Foam dots
- Hot-glue gun and glue sticks

- String
- Trim
- Variety of embellishments including miniature paper flowers
- Variety of ephemera including photos, trinkets, ticket stubs, maps, postcards, etc.

Directions

1. After choosing a theme for the shadowbox, such as a child's first year of school, a birthday, holiday, honeymoon, or vacation, begin selecting your largest and most favorite paper image or photo for the background.

2. Arrange a scene using ephemera, and glue items in place.

Hankie Picture Frame

Many vintage hankies come with pretty print, embroidered, or cross-stitched borders. They are perfect for adding a feminine, vintage feel to photo frame mat boards. By adding a ribbon for hanging and a few millinery flowers at the top, we have a lovely frame—perfect for you or a good friend.

Materials

- Photo frame mat board cut to the size of the hankie
- Coordinating ribbon
- Craft knife
- Decorative hankie with a nice border
- Cutting mat
- Fabric adhesive
- Fabric scissors
- Millinery flowers
- Spray adhesive
- Thin-gauge wire (optional)
- Wire cutters (optional)

Dena's Tip

If you can't find a mat board that fits the size of your hankie, you can cut your own, using a mat or craft knife and cutting mat.

Directions

1. Apply spray adhesive to wrong side of hankie in a well-ventilated space. Firmly smooth hankie to right side of mat board.

2. Turn board over onto the cutting mat and cut an X in the board opening from corner to corner.

3. Trim and glue edges back approximately 1" on all sides.

4. Using the fabric adhesive, attach two lengths of ribbon to the top of the mat to form a hanger. Tie at the top with a knot or bow.

5. Place millinery flowers onto ribbon at the bow. If the flowers aren't already wired, attach them to the ribbon with wire.

Salt and Pepper Shaker Tassels

My friend Karen originally taught me how to make this project. By experimenting, I found an easier way to achieve the same results. If you can't find a whimsical shaker, a hat-pin holder will work. All you need is a small vintage figurine or salt and pepper shaker that has at least two holes at the top and one hole at the bottom.

The bullion fringe comes in a wide variety of colors and since you only need a few special beads, splurge on those.

Dena's Tip

Look for single salt or pepper shakers—they're less expensive than a pair.

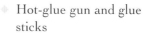

Materials

- Salt shaker, preferably vintage
- 1 yard cotton bullion fringe
- 26-gauge wire
- Beads in a variety of sizes
- Fabric adhesive
- Hot-glue gun and glue sticks
- Small-tipped scissors
- Variety of decorative trims
- Washcloth
- Wire cutters

Directions

1. Cut a piece of wire approximately 12" long. Thread wire through one of the holes at the top of the shaker and through the bottom hole, so that you have approximately 4" at the bottom.

2. Thread a small bead (one that won't slip into the shaker hole), a medium-size bead, a large bead, and another medium-size bead onto the wire.

3. Thread tiny beads onto the wire until you have enough to create a loop.

4. Thread another large bead onto the wire, then thread the wire through the other hole at the top of the shaker and through the bottom hole. You should now have both ends of the wire coming through the bottom hole.

5. Twist the two wire ends together until they hold the beaded area firmly in place.

6. Trim the wires, then hot-glue them to the bottom of the shaker.

7. Place a line of fabric adhesive along the top edge of the bullion fringe, then roll the fringe up tightly. Continue rolling the fringe until it is the same diameter as the bottom of the shaker—making a perfect tassel.

8. Hot-glue the tassel onto the bottom of the shaker and hold it in place until it dries.

9. Wrap trim around the top of the tassel where it meets the shaker. Add additional trim as desired.

10. Loop a small piece of trim through the beaded loop to hang.

Ribbon Switch Plate Covers

Let's face it, plastic switch-plate covers are boring and not terribly attractive. Even in upscale home boutiques, I rarely find a pretty one. They are perfect for embellishing. Using two different trims, you can get a simple striped pattern. For something a bit more elaborate, use a variety of trims and ribbons.

An alternative to the Ribbon Switch Plate Covers project is to use fabric instead of ribbons. A nice sturdy fabric like velvet is perfect because it's thick enough that the plastic will not show underneath. It's fast and easy, and is a great way to tie in the coordinating colors in any room.

Materials

◆ Plastic switch plate

◆ Craft knife

◆ Craft scissors

◆ Cutting board

◆ Double-sided permanent adhesive sheet

◆ Fabric adhesive

◆ Fabric scissors

◆ Ribbon flower

◆ Variety of ribbons of different widths

Dena's Tip

Lay your ribbons out before you adhere them to your switch plate. Make sure the colors and patterns work well together and that you have enough trim to cover the entire plate.

Note: Double-sided permanent adhesive sheets are available at crafts stores and are usually used for adhering micro-beads to crafts projects. They are extra sticky and are backed on both sides with paper, so they come in handy for all kinds of projects.

Directions

1. Cut all ribbons ½" longer than the width of the switch plate.

2. Cut a piece of double-sided adhesive sheet slightly larger than the switch plate. Snip the four corners on an angle. Peel paper off one side of the adhesive sheet and apply to the front of the switch plate. Wrap edges around the back of the switch plate.

3. Peel off remaining side of adhesive sheet. Adhere the ribbons down the front of the switch plate one at a time, leaving ¼" on each side of the ribbon. Make sure the ribbons meet each other but don't overlap.

4. Fold ribbon edges under the plate.

5. Turn the switch plate over and use a craft knife to cut an X in the opening for the switch. Fold under.

6. Use the craft knife to cut the openings for the screws.

7. Using fabric adhesive, attach the ribbon flower to the front of the switch plate wherever desired.

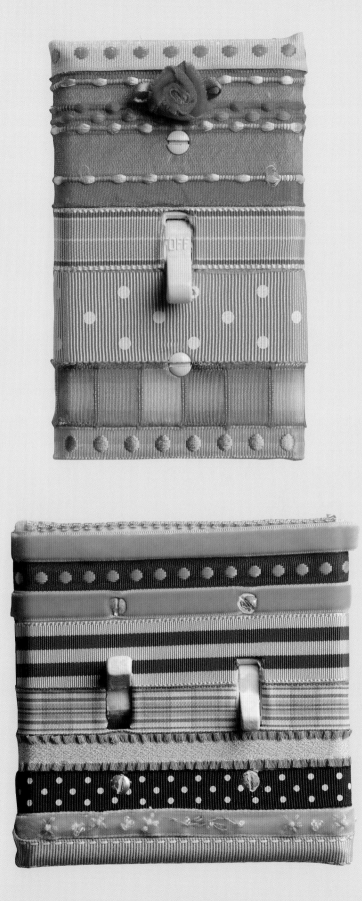

Wall Decor

When I planned the color and design scheme of my home, I visualized the entire house, not just a single room. It's important that colors and styles flow from one room to the next to create harmony throughout the home. In my house, we have a lot of soft blues, yellows, and greens—colors that work well together. Every room isn't a carbon copy of the next, however. Some themes carry over: I have florals in a few rooms and geometrics in another, and in some I have both. That combination ties it all together.

The projects in this chapter focus on wall art. They range from simple to elaborate and all are fun to create. Depending on the decor in your home, you can go from whimsical to romantic, from vintage to modern, or from country to old-world. It's up to you.

Sunroom Plates

I've been collecting plates for almost 20 years. I adore them. They are like framed works of art. The border is the frame and the intricate interior is the painting. Over the years, my collection has grown. In my home, they are grouped around windows, door-ways, and on beams. They add charm and warmth to any room of your home.

Materials

- Variety of vintage plates
- Hammer
- Hanging nails
- Wire plate holders

Directions

1. Attach plates to wire plate holders. Secure nails into wall, then hang the plates.

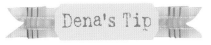
Dena's Tip

Try hanging 5–7 plates over a doorway. It will make a very pretty statement.

Dining Room

We painted our dining room at least five times. We were just going to pick a solid color, but nothing seemed quite right, so we ended up painting a decorative pattern on the walls. I chose to paint swirls, leaves, and berries, then outlined everything with a vibrant gold acrylic for a touch of elegance. This is a more time-consuming project for the experienced painter, but well worth the effort. And remember—if you don't like it, you can always paint over it!

Dena's Tip

When painting walls, lightly pencil in the pattern. Then start painting one color before moving on to the next. This saves lots of time.

Materials

- Acrylic paints in a variety of colors, including metallic gold
- Eraser
- Latex paints in a light color for base and a complementary darker color
- Paint roller
- Paintbrushes in a variety of sizes
- Pencil
- Sandpaper in fine grit

Directions

1. Paint the base color with a roller and let dry.

2. Using a pencil and a light hand, map out desired design on the walls.

3. Paint the design and let dry.

4. Using the complementary shade, paint in between all of the elements, leaving some of the background shade showing, which will appear as an outline around the designs. Let paint dry.

5. Using a medium round brush, outline all of the elements in metallic gold. Let paint dry.

6. Erase all pencil marks.

7. Lightly sand the walls for an aged look.

Guest Bathroom

I tackled this bathroom in stages. As new ideas came to me, I'd add them. First, I did the walls in a green finish, then added the roses. Next, I painted the border and lattice design. A few weeks later, I decided the ceiling needed something, so I added rubber-stamped gold leaves. Stamping is much easier and faster than painting a ceiling—and you will be so happy with the results.

Dena's Tip

Try your colors and finishes on small 8"-square boards before you tackle an entire wall. It will save you a lot of time in the long run.

Materials

- Damp gauze fabric, cut into large squares
- Damp kitchen sponges
- Eggshell-finish acrylic or latex paints in a variety of colors including gold metallic
- Gold ink pad
- Large plastic disposable cups
- Paintbrushes in a variety of sizes
- Pencil
- Rubber stamp
- Ruler
- Sandpapers in fine and medium grits
- Water

Directions

1. In a large plastic cup, mix background paints to desired color. Add water to paint mixture to get a creamy consistency.

2. Apply paint with damp gauze and damp kitchen sponge. The technique is a lot like washing the walls. Add more color in some areas and remove some color in other areas by wiping off the paint. Let paint dry.

3. Add other colors for more depth, if desired. Let paint dry.

4. Add flowers to walls. Practice drawing rose bouquets on paper or canvas first, then lightly pencil in the location of the bouquets.

5. If desired, add a chair-rail border and gold lattice pattern on the bottom. Lightly pencil in the location of the chair rail. Use a ruler for straight lines in the lattice design.

6. Stamp ceiling with rubber stamp and gold ink. Add the stamped pattern on the walls as well, if desired, to tie them in with the ceiling. Let everything dry.

7. For an aged look, lightly rub sandpaper over the flowers.

Rachel's Room

My daughter Rachel wanted a makeover for her room a few years ago. We decided to give her room the feeling of a bed-and-breakfast inn. Rachel chose the pretty blue background color, then I got to work painting the flowers.

Dena's Tip

We wanted to keep the ceiling nice and easy, so we went with a striped wallpaper, which coordinated nicely with the rest of the patterns.

Materials

- Acrylic paints in brown, cream, light and dark green, light and dark pink, red, and soft buttery yellow
- Craft sticks
- Dinner-size paper plate, cut in half
- Eraser
- Large plastic disposable cups
- Latex paint in blue or desired base color
- Paintbrushes
- Paper towels
- Pencil

Directions

1. Paint two coats of base color on walls. Let paint dry.

2. Create a scalloped border at the top of the walls. For a template, place the flat edge of the paper plate against the ceiling and using a pencil, trace all around the plate. Continue this all the way around the room.

3. Draw in little leaf patterns on each side of the scalloped lines to form a pretty design.

4. Between each scallop, by the top of the ceiling, draw a simple flower.

5. Using a pencil, map out spacing of the bouquets all over the walls. Space them fairly evenly.

6. Using acrylic paints, fill everything in. Paint one color at a time and go from light to dark. Use cream, light and dark pink, and a touch of red for the flowers. Use yellow for the centers of the flowers and brown for flower outlines. Use light and dark green for the leaves.

Diamond Entry

Each one of us has a decorating horror story to tell. I remember crying over this particular project. We had primed the walls of our entryway, painted the topcoat, and painted the diamonds. We even outlined each one in gold. Thinking the project was finished, I went shopping. When I came home all the colors had run and the walls had a mud-like quality. My husband had tried waxing the walls, a technique that had worked for us in the past. We realized too late, however, that this time he had used the wrong type of wax.

Thankfully, this was just paint. So after everything dried, we painted again, and now it looks great. I'm very happy with the way it turned out. I know looking back years from now, we can laugh—sort of!

Dena's Tip

If you're using multiple colors, test them out on paper first. You can also add white paint to half of each one to get additional shades.

Materials

- Acrylic paints in at least 8 colors, including gold metallic, and watered down to a creamy consistency
- Eraser
- Foam brushes
- Medium-size round brush
- Pencil
- Straightedge ruler

Directions

1. Draw diamonds on walls with ruler and pencil. To achieve a hand-painted look, don't mask them off with painter's tape.

2. Using foam brushes, paint diamonds in random colors. Let paint dry.

3. Using gold acrylic paint and a round brush, paint a wavy line around each diamond. This will hide all imperfections and give extra detail to your diamond pattern.

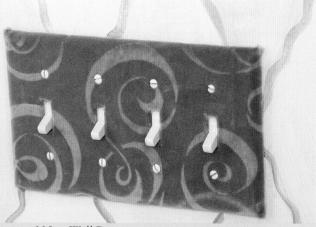

Hand-drawn Frames on Walls

Drawing on the walls with a permanent marker is not for everyone, but I love the look I get with it. Just make sure you pencil it in first and love it before you go to the point of no return. You can practice on a piece of paper first.

For this project, I visualized drawing frames on my walls for all the frameless paintings I have purchased at flea markets. You can also draw frames around plain mirrors, wall sconces, and wherever else strikes your fancy.

Materials

◆ Fine-point permanent marker

◆ Pencil

◆ Ruler

Directions

1. Using a ruler, draw a light border around your artwork in pencil.

2. Lightly draw a swirly border around artwork.

3. Go over pencil swirls with marker.

Dena's Tip

Markers also work well on furniture. I once used an ultrafine-point gold marker to draw a border on my bathroom cabinets. It turned out beautifully.

Hallway

Simple stripes are a lovely solution for many rooms. The nice thing about painting them yourself is that you can choose your own colors, whereas wallpaper is a bit limiting. For a first-time project, I would suggest two colors: the lighter color will be painted all over the walls and the darker color will be the stripe.

Dena's Tip

Try stripes in varying widths if you have more time and you're feeling daring. Bar-code-like stripes are popular right now. Try them horizontally or vertically.

Materials

- Foam brushes
- Glaze
- Latex paints in a light color for base and a complementary darker color
- Painter's tape
- Sea sponge

Directions

1. Paint the wall in base color. Let paint dry. Mask off the stripes with painter's tape.

2. Mix one part darker paint to four parts glaze and apply the paint/glaze mixture with a foam brush between the painter's tape. Dab with sea sponge.

3. Let paint dry, then remove tape.

Storage

For those of us who love to embellish, being organized and clutter-free is a must. That's why storing our prized possessions is so necessary. You might find a special treasure at a flea market or crafts store. Keeping supplies and embellishments—assorted fabrics, pieces of jewelry, trims, various papers, and other keepsakes—in order makes planning and carrying out a project a joy. With everything at your fingertips, you will save time.

This section is filled with beautiful storage containers that you will want to display in your home. Some make great gifts. The trick is to make it personal and enjoy the design process. The containers will be as special as the treasures they hold.

Storage Boxes

I love keeping my supplies organized in pretty containers. Sometimes it is hard to find the perfect container that goes with your style and decor. So instead of spending lots of time searching for that perfect box, why not embellish one and come up with your own?

I chose some pretty aqua boxes for this project because of their lovely color, sturdiness, and simple design—making them perfect for embellishing. These boxes also came as a nested set of three, but you can choose boxes in different shapes and sizes.

Dena's Tip

You can purchase a special polka-dot magic marker at a crafts store.

Materials

- Square storage box
- ¼"-wide black rickrack
- Alphabet rubber stamps
- Clear craft glue
- Craft scissors
- Crystal glitter
- Decoupage medium
- Fabric adhesive
- Foam brush
- Gold ink pad
- Large black polka-dot marker
- Vintage clipart of frames or borders
- Vintage flowers

Directions

1. Apply dots all over the box with polka-dot marker. Let marker dry.
2. Measure rickrack around the lid of the box and cut. Glue rickrack around the box lid with fabric adhesive.
3. Stamp the name of box's contents on clipart frame. Apply decoupage medium with the foam brush to the back side of frame and adhere to box.
4. Assemble vintage flowers in a pleasing arrangement and glue them onto the top of the box lid with fabric adhesive.
5. Apply clear glue to the tips of flowers and before the glue dries, sprinkle the glued area with glitter. Shake off any excess.

Jewelry Rack

Don't hide your jewelry inside a box—display it! My jewelry rack is hanging in my bathroom. I use it for mostly vintage costume jewelry.

Materials

- Plain wooden peg rack
- Chenille yarn
- Craft knife
- Cutting mat
- Fabric adhesive
- Hot-glue gun and glue sticks
- Pencil
- Picture hanger
- Spray adhesive
- Variety of embellishments, such as costume jewelry or buttons, for top of each peg
- Wallpaper border, preferably vintage

Important note: The ribbon hanger at the top is just a decorative touch. I place a picture hanger on the back of the pegboard to support the weight with the jewelry on it.

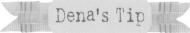
Dena's Tip

For a vintage look, use an inexpensive chenille ribbon as a border. You can also cover the peg rack with a vintage wallpaper border.

Directions

1. Measure and cut the wallpaper border to fit the front of peg rack.

2. Holding wallpaper on top of pegs, mark the center of each peg with a pencil.

3. Cut an X with the craft knife at each penciled mark.

4. In a well-ventilated area, spray the adhesive onto the wrong side of the wallpaper border. Pushing pegs through X cuts, adhere the border to the peg rack. Smooth out any air bubbles.

5. Use fabric adhesive and chenille yarn to cover any exposed wood areas.

6. Hot-glue different embellishments to the front of each peg. The embellishments can be all the same. If you choose a variety, make sure they have a flat surface for gluing and that they coordinate in color or theme.

7. If desired, add a decorative ribbon at the top to create the appearance of a ribbon hanger.

8. Place picture hanger on the back of the peg rack and hang on wall.

Hangtags for Glass Storage Jars

Large glass storage jars are great for holding everything from buttons to change. I like hanging a whimsical tag with a metal chain around the neck of the jar. It gives it a vintage feel and the label can be easily changed.

You can find metal frames for tags in a scrapbook store or crafts shop. They come in a variety of styles and shapes.

Dena's Tip

The metal ball chain can be purchased in a variety of places. I purchase mine by the foot or yard at a local hardware store.

Materials

- Large glass jar
- Alphabet stickers or alphabet rubber stamps with black ink pad
- Light metal pull chain, enough to hang around storage jar with a bit extra
- Mini metal frame
- Scrapbook paper
- White craft glue
- Wire
- Wire cutters

Directions

1. Cut a piece of scrapbook paper to fit inside the metal frame.
2. Stamp or adhere letters to paper to spell out storage jar contents.
3. Using white glue, adhere label to the back of the frame.
4. Attach pull chain with a bit of wire or glue.
5. Hang tag around storage jar.

Ribbon Photo Album

I collect lovely ribbons of all shapes, colors, and sizes. I don't wait until I have a specific project in mind—if I love them, I know they will be used in the near future. For this project, I had a great time mixing florals, checkers, stripes, and polka dots. I'm sure you will, too.

Materials

- Small photo album with cut-out window
- Craft scissors
- Embellishment to adhere to the inside window
- Hot-glue gun and glue sticks
- Strong double-sided tape
- Variety of color-coordinated ribbons and trims, enough to cover front of album

Dena's Tip

Use a combination of velvet and embroidered ribbons to create a rich and elegant design.

Directions

1. Cut ribbons and trims to cover the front of album, leaving ½" on both sides to tuck under. Lay them out in desired pattern.
2. Adhere double-sided tape to the wrong side of the trim and ribbon. Starting at the top of the album and working down, adhere ribbon and trim to album, one piece at a time. Make sure you don't cover the window of the album.
3. Hot-glue embellishment to the center of the window.

Hankie Photo Album

I love vintage hankies—the beautiful borders, the lovely cotton, and the nostalgic feelings they evoke in me. It's so much fun to find them at flea markets, thrift shops, and garage sales. Vintage handkerchiefs give this project an old-world feel. You can use an old photo album that needs a facelift or find a plain, inexpensive one at a discount store, crafts shop, or flea market.

Dena's Tip

I love to personalize gifts and projects for myself and for friends. You can do the same by writing a brief message, a friend's name, or a sweet sentiment on a ribbon and attaching it to a paper bouquet that you place in a hankie "pocket."

Materials

- Photo album approximately the same size as hankies
- 2 hankies
- Fabric adhesive
- Fabric scissors
- Spray adhesive
- Tiny paper flower bouquet

Directions

1. Cut one hankie to fit the front of the album. Using fabric adhesive, glue down the raw edges.

2. Using spray adhesive, spray the back of hankie. Adhere to the front of the photo album and smooth out any bubbles.

3. Cut a corner from the second hankie to form a triangle. This will be the pocket that you place on the front of photo album.

4. Glue the raw edge under with fabric adhesive and glue the pocket to the front of the album on two sides. Keep the top open to form a pocket.

5. Place the tiny bouquet into the pocket and adhere.

Tin Container

Why cover perfection? The classic tin can is quite chic. The shiny silver surface works in many settings, from vintage to modern. The ridges on the container can be enhanced with metallic rickrack and other embellishments. I found nuts at the hardware store that I used as "feet" on one of the containers in my studio. The shape was perfect and they were inexpensive.

Dena's Tip

Take a trip to the hardware store to find unusual, inexpensive, and interesting metal embellishments such as wire, nuts, and bolts.

Materials

- 28-oz. tin can
- 1½"-wide metallic ribbon
- 24" piece of 18- or 20-gauge bailing wire
- Fabric adhesive
- Hammer
- Hardware nuts
- Hot-glue gun and glue sticks
- Metallic embroidered medallion as centerpiece
- Metallic rickrack
- Nail
- Pencil
- Wire cutters
- Wood block
- Wood-colored floral spray

Directions

1. Remove the can's label and wash the inside and outside.
2. Using the wood block to hammer onto, hammer a nail into each side of top of can for handle holes, from the inside out.
3. Coil the center part of the wire around a pencil to create a handle. Leave approximately 5" on each end. Loosen the coiled handle a little and pull it off the pencil.
4. Thread each end of wire, from the outside in, and bend wire up over the edge and down on outside of the can. Snip the extra off with wire cutters.
5. Using fabric adhesive, glue wide ribbon around the center of the can.
6. Starting in the back, use fabric adhesive to glue rickrack around the top and bottom of the can.
7. Hot-glue the medallion onto the wide ribbon in the center.
8. Hot-glue three nuts to the bottom of the can, spacing them evenly.
9. Spray with wood-colored floral spray for an aged look.

A Note from the Author

I can't remember when I first started embellishing. It seems like I was born collecting things that caught my eye and finding ways to make them new, different—mine. I like to have furniture and accessories that have my own stamp on it. I also love the process. It's an adventure shopping at flea markets, hardware stores, crafts shops, and yard sales. I'm always on the lookout for my next great find, and I never know where it will turn up. Because reorganizing a good piece for embellishing takes vision, the search engages the imagination as much as the project itself does.

I also love the fact that my family has joined in. We have a lot of fun hunting for treasures, and it's as rewarding to spend the time together as it is to share our creativity.

With the art of embellishing, anyone can become his or her own designer. You can save money while creating things that are truly special. I hope I have helped you find ways to show your personality, beautify your surroundings, and create gifts from the heart. This, after all, is what embellishing is all about.

About the Author

"Embellish your life" is Dena Fishbein's motto. Star of her own television show, *Embellish This!*, on the DIY (Do It Yourself) network and creative director of Dena Designs, Inc., Dena's mission is to transform the ordinary into the extraordinary. Currently airing several times a week, *Embellish This!* is a hit for the DIY network. Dena has developed a publishing program on embellishing to share her talents. She also writes a monthly syndicated newspaper column on design.

Winner of 17 Louis awards as well as the Greeting Card of the Year award from the National Greeting Card Association, Dena has a passion for embellishing. She has developed her own signature style through her company, Dena Designs, Inc., which produces dinnerware and giftware, infant and juvenile bedding and accessories, stationery, fabrics, and home accessories.

Dena's husband and business partner, Dan, and their three children also share her love of embellishing. According to Dena, "Embellishing is about having fun, spending only a little, laughing a whole lot, and ending up with something you just love."

Acknowledgments

So many thanks! Thank you, Jo, for believing in me and being the loveliest publisher a girl could ever want. To Cindy S., thanks for ironing out the wrinkles. To Michelle, Lisa, and Jenn, thanks for your infinite patience and writing expertise. Thank you thank you thank you, Heidi, for being the wonderful, dedicated, and creative graphic designer that you are. Thank you, Sara, for keeping us all on track. (And thank you, Wendy, for having such "mahvelous" daughters.) Thank you, Rose, for making me laugh and laugh and laugh. Swaggy thanks you, too, and appreciates his MVP status. Yo, yo, yo, Suzie, you know you're the best. Thanks to all my friends, I love you all. Most of all, thank you to my best friend and husband Danny, my children David, Rachel, and Lisa, M&M, D&A, I love you more than the whole wide world.

Dena

Metric Conversion Chart

inches to millimeters and centimeters

inches	mm	cm	inches	cm	inches	cm
⅛	3	0.3	9	22.9	30	76.2
¼	6	0.6	10	25.4	31	78.7
½	13	1.3	12	30.5	33	83.8
⅝	16	1.6	13	33.0	34	86.4
¾	19	1.9	14	35.6	35	88.9
⅞	22	2.2	15	38.1	36	91.4
1	25	2.5	16	40.6	37	94.0
1¼	32	3.2	17	43.2	38	96.5
1½	38	3.8	18	45.7	39	99.1
1¾	44	4.4	19	48.3	40	101.6
2	51	5.1	20	50.8	41	104.1
2½	64	6.4	21	53.3	42	106.7
3	76	7.6	22	55.9	43	109.2
3½	89	8.9	23	58.4	44	111.8
4	102	10.2	24	61.0	45	114.3
4½	114	11.4	25	63.5	46	116.8
5	127	12.7	26	66.0	47	119.4
6	152	15.2	27	68.6	48	121.9
7	178	17.8	28	71.1	49	124.5
8	203	20.3	29	73.7	50	127.0

yards to meters

yards	meters	yards	meters	yards	meters	yards	meters	yards	meters
⅛	0.11	2⅛	1.94	4⅛	3.77	6⅛	5.60	8⅛	7.43
⅛	0.11	2⅛	1.94	4⅛	3.77	6⅛	5.60	8⅛	7.43
¼	0.23	2¼	2.06	4¼	3.89	6¼	5.72	8¼	7.54
⅜	0.34	2⅜	2.17	4⅜	4.00	6⅜	5.83	8⅜	7.66
⅝	0.46	2½	2.29	4½	4.11	6½	5.94	8½	7.77
⅝	0.57	2⅝	2.40	4⅝	4.23	6⅝	6.06	8⅝	7.89
¾	0.69	2¾	2.51	4¾	4.34	6¾	6.17	8¾	8.00
⅞	0.80	2⅞	2.63	4⅞	4.46	6⅞	6.29	8⅞	8.12
1	0.91	3	2.74	5	4.57	7	6.40	9	8.23
1¼	1.03	3¼	2.86	5⅛	4.69	7¼	6.52	9⅛	8.34
1¼	1.14	3¼	2.97	5¼	4.80	7¼	6.63	9¼	8.46
1⅜	1.26	3⅜	3.09	5⅜	4.91	7⅜	6.74	9⅜	8.57
1½	1.37	3½	3.20	5½	5.03	7½	6.86	9½	8.69
1⅝	1.49	3⅝	3.31	5⅝	5.14	7⅝	6.97	9⅝	8.80
1¾	1.60	3¾	3.43	5¾	5.26	7¾	7.09	9¾	8.92
1⅞	1.71	3⅞	3.54	5⅞	5.37	7⅞	7.20	9⅞	9.03
2	1.83	4	3.66	6	5.49	8	7.32	10	9.14

Index